Recorder For Beginners

Practical Music Guide To Learn How To Play The Recorder Notes And Tunes, Including Easy Popular Songs

Ben Newman

Recorder for Beginners.. 6

How is made Recorder... **8**

How To Hold your Recorder.. **9**

How to Place your Fingers 11

How to blow into your instrument **13**

Tips and Tricks **14**

Let's Start Playing ! **19**

The Fingering Chart **22**

How to Play Notes **24**

C 24

Low D 25

Low E.. 25

Low F 26

F# (F sharp) 26

G... 27

A 27

Bb... 28

B 28

C'.. 29

D... 29

Rhythm.. **30**

Examples 34

Bar lines 35

Musi 35

cal Rules 36

Mapping between musical notation and Tablature fingering position 37

Time To Practice **38**

Song Book... **44**

Happy Birthday.. 44

Twinkle, Twinkle Little Star... 45

Row Row Row Your Boat.. 46

Frere Jacques 47

The Old Gray Mare 48

The Muffin Man 49

There's a Hole in the Bucket... 50

This Old Man 51

Hush, Little Baby... 52

Mary Had a Little Lamb... 53

London Bridge 54

Old Mac Donald Had a Farm *55*
Finger Chart Overview *56*

Care your Recorder **57**
Conclusion **59**

Introduction

The recorder is usually taught to children while they're young but it's not classified as a child's instrument. There is a great deal of difficult and complex music written for the recorder since it was around before the flute or at least the modern transverse flute. For high-quality wood recorders that are played by professionals and have a soft warm sound sound that is unmatched by the plastic version. Those recorders also cost upwards of thousands of dollars.

A recorder is an instrument that most people learn how to play in school and it's a very versatile instrument that makes beautiful music and most people find it very enjoyable to play.

In this book you'll be learning everything you need to know about a recorder and we have songs at the end of the book that are easy to learn and easy to play.

This book is perfect for beginners people; it teaches the basic for beginners and to start playing the 6 holes Soprano Recorder

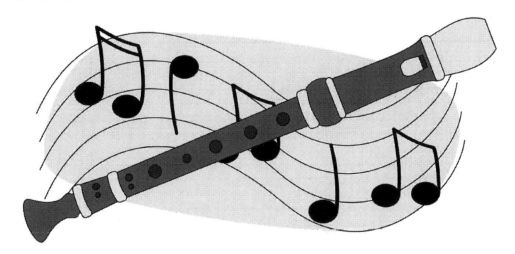

People who are just starting out on the recorder, don't need an instrument of thousand dollars, because they can simply use the plastic instrument until they become professionals.

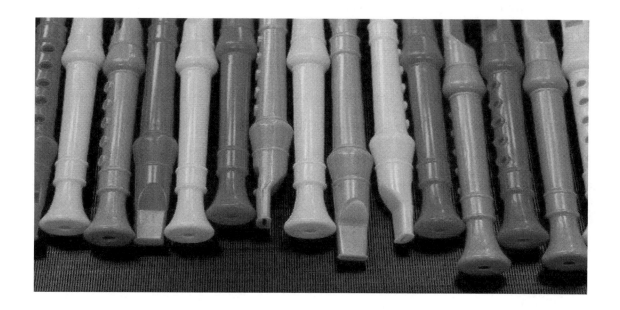

They may look like toys but they are not. Many of them are precision instruments with a very high-quality sound. The plastic recorders are made from a resin known as ABS which is the same polymer that is used in the bumper of a car. This makes the recorder less subject to having damage or wear on it. Plastic recorders can also be submerged in water for cleaning where a wood recorder or an ivory recorder obviously would not be able to do that. A wooden recorder has a nicer sound because wood is a natural polymer called cellulose. As such it is more in need of care and no water whatsoever is allowed near a wood recorder. A wood recorder needs to be oiled on the inside to protect it from moisture which can damage the wood. If the wood gets damaged then it can dry out and crack.

A plastic recorder will also need an oil called recorder cream and this is a petroleum based product that is similar to Vaseline and you place it on the joint so that the recorder pieces can be more easily put together and take it apart just as easily. This is also so that the joints will seal properly.

Oils and the lubricants that are used on the recorder should be made from natural or synthetic polymers. They come in a variety of sizes varying from a tiny soprano to a great bass or a massive bass and the larger instruments you will notice have plastic or metal keys and pads to cover the holes. The reason for this is that the holes are too far apart for your fingers and this is why the keys operate like an oboe or clarinet and the pads that cover the holes are generally made from beginners kin or leather.

How is made Recorder

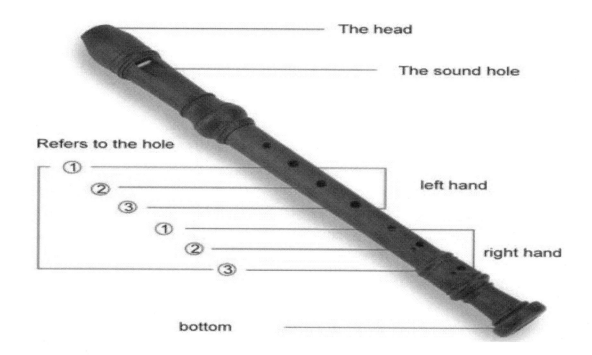

The head

The sound hole

Refers to the hole

① ② ③

① ② ③

left hand

right hand

bottom

You will notice that a recorder has a headpiece called the head joint. This is the very top piece of the instrument. There is a mouthpiece where you will blow air into the instrument to make sound. A window is below the mouthpiece and the window is where the sound will come out at least in part. There are also finger holes and this is where you will stick your fingers over the holes to produce different sounds. At the bottom there is a foot joint and this is at the very end of the instrument. The foot joint has a hole in the middle so this will help your sound produce as well and it will be clear.

Every recorder looks a lot like flute but it's not one. One of the oldest members of the flute family is what it actually is. It dates back to the Renaissance times and even before then. It also works like a modern flute in many aspects but the air is blown through it instead of across it.

How To Hold your Recorder

This chapter will be explaining how you hold it and where your fingers need to go as well as how to blow into the instrument and then how to care for it because you don't want your instrument breaking on you or having damage done to it. Plastic recorders may be cheaper to buy but that doesn't mean that they are super cheap to buy. You don't want to spend more than you have to.

- **All recorders have a thumb hole** in the back and they have seven holes down the front of the instrument. Some also have double holes on the bottom which means that there will be two holes on the bottom if this is what is on your instrument.

- **The left hand** is going to need to be placed at the top of the recorder by the mouthpiece. Remember that the mouthpiece is at the top where your going to be blowing your air. The left hand is going to cover the thumb hole in the back and the first three holes so your pinky of your left hand is never used and you should hold it away from the instrument.

- **Your right hand** is going to be placed at the bottom of the recorder and you need to place you're right thumb in place to be used to balance the instrument and is going to be placed between the fourth and fifth holes on the back. The right hand fingers are going to cover the four holes near the bottom of your instrument and you will need to make sure that you're covering the holes completely with the flat pad of your finger.

- **Do not use your fingertips.** Use that flashy pad at the end of your finger but not the fingertip. Your fingers when holding this instrument should be slightly curved and your fingers that are not being used to cover the holes should be held a little distance above the holes so that they are ready to quickly play the next note.

- **Hold your recorder at a 45° angle** and your elbows should be slightly away from your body and it is important to make sure that you're sitting up straight.

How to Place your Fingers

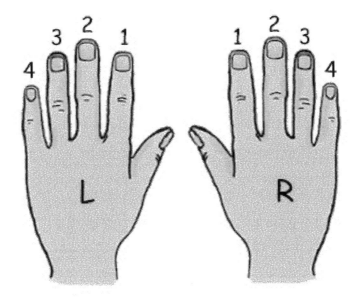

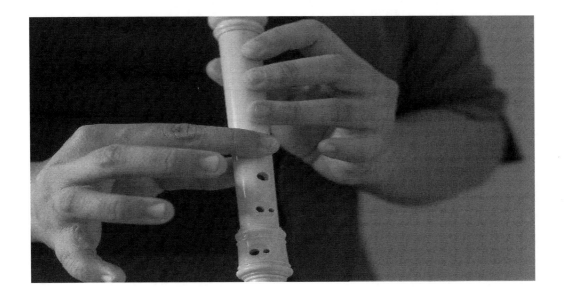

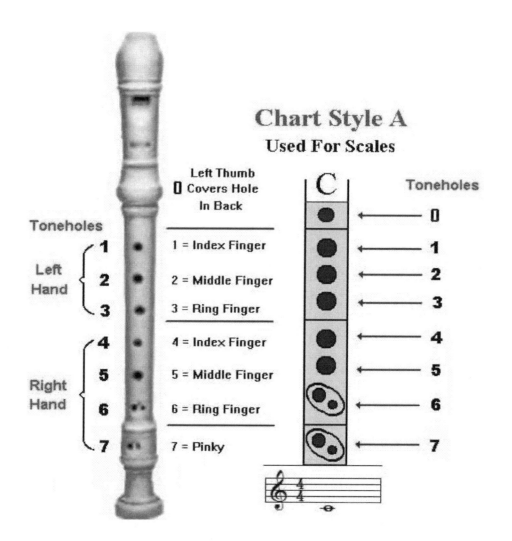

Chart Style A
Used For Scales

Tonoholes

Left Hand
- 1
- 2
- 3

Right Hand
- 4
- 5
- 6
- 7

0 Left Thumb Covers Hole In Back

1 = Index Finger

2 = Middle Finger

3 = Ring Finger

4 = Index Finger

5 = Middle Finger

6 = Ring Finger

7 = Pinky

C

Tonoholes
- 0
- 1
- 2
- 3
- 4
- 5
- 6
- 7

How to blow into your instrument

This is a process that is going to be taken seriously because if you blow the wrong way or if you have the recorder in the wrong position you can damage your instrument.

1) **Place the tip of the recorder into your mouth**. What you need to remember here is that you're going to play the recorder but you do not want to eat it. So you never want to have the recorder so far in your mouth that your teeth are touching the mouthpiece and digging into the wood or the plastic. Obviously if your teeth are digging into the wood or the plastic of the instrument it's not going to work the way needs to and you could end up having to replace the head joint. You just want your mouth to be on the tip. If your teeth are touching the mouthpiece than you have the recorder too far into your mouth and you will need to move the recorder outward so that only your lips are around the mouthpiece.

2) **Blow gently**. The recorder is a very small woodwind instrument it is not a bigger instrument that is going to need more air such as a tuba or a bigger instrument. If you try to blow as much air into this instrument as you do into other instruments that are larger, you won't end up producing the sound that you want. The sound that will come out is going to be a sound that will be loud and it will squeak. You will be putting too much air in the instrument, which is why it's going to be squeaking and you could damage the instrument as well.

Tips and Tricks

1) **Tonguing your notes**: another trick to using your instrument properly is that you will be tonguing your notes.

   Tonguing your notes sounds very odd and you're probably thinking 'how do I tongue my notes'? To produce a clear beginning to each note you need to learn to use your tongue to begin and separate each note. The tip of your tongue should gently touch the back of your upper teeth at the point where the gum meets your front teeth. This is the same process you would use when you're saying the word do. You may find it easier to practice by saying the word do. So practice by saying do do do until you gain a feel for the concepts and you can produce the same action with only your air but no sound.

2) **Avoid Squeaking**: squeaking is one of the most frustrating things about beginning to play the recorder and it is something that beginners will experience and frequently in some cases.

   Something that you should remember is that you're just starting out and that squeaking will happen. It's not a bad thing. It is a normal part of learning to play an instrument and you shouldn't worry too much about whether or not your instrument is squeaking. It is going to happen at some point.

   However, there are many different ways that we can stop this from happening or help it to not happen as much. Whether it's continuous or occasional, squeaks can ruin a good song but fortunately you can get past this because there are three main components of this, and it's bubbles, air or your fingers. They all cause the same issues to your instrument and if we can avoid this problem you'll be able to minimize this issue. Very very easy tips for avoiding this or making it better and will be listing them here

aky fingers are common and cause squeaking commonly as well. In order to combat this you must make sure that your fingers are completely sealing the hole. Remember not to use your fingertips but use the fleshy pad that's at the tip of your finger. You also need to make sure that you're playing with flat fingers and never curved ones. Imagine that you're being fingerprinted and when you're being fingerprinted you know that you have to flatten your fingertips.

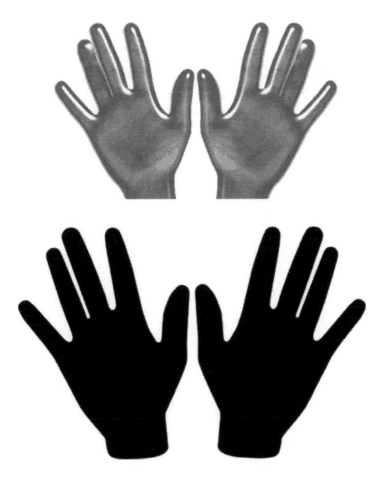

Depending on the size of your hand, the tips of your fingers will either hang over the side of your recorder or reach the holes. In either situation, your fingers should be able to cover the holes but it may be a little difficult. So you may need practice holding it and covering the holes. Squeaks can also occur when you're changing notes because this is due to one of your fingers moving enough to barely seal a hole. In most cases when this happens it's usually the left thumb or your first finger that is moving. This is where practice involving the moving between notes is going to help train your fingers not to move.

3) **Avoid Bubbles**: another problem is bubbles. Occasionally, you will get a small condensation bubble that could've been trapped in your mouthpiece and this will usually occur after you have been blowing on your recorder for a long period of time or a significant amount of time. This is usually for around a quarter of an hour and what this does is it will cause your instrument to squeak as a result. To clear the bubble, you need to place the recorder in your mouth as if you were about to play, but instead of blowing, you need to inhale. This is because it is going to suck the air up through the recorder instead of being blown down through it. So you need to suck the air into your mouth and as a result the bubble will be gone.

4) **Air:** the last problem is air. If your fingers are sealing the holes tight and you're still squeaking, then you're probably blowing too hard. You need to think that you want to blow softly. Almost like you're whispering to the recorder when you're playing. You want the recorder to sound like a whisper. You also want to check that you don't have too much of the mouthpiece in your

mouth. As we said above you do not want to touch your teeth. Just place it in between your lips. If the tip of the mouthpiece is too far in, it's going to cause squeaking as well. Following these tips will help you be able to keep the squeaking at a minimum.

This is really important when you're learning how to play your instrument and you're trying to keep the squeaking down and to a minimum. You need to make sure that bubbles and air or not affecting your instrument but you also need to make sure that your fingers aren't harming how you play either. If they aren't over the holes properly, your instrument won't make the notes play the proper way. The notes will squeak instead.

It can be very difficult to play an instrument when your fingers are not in the proper positioning or if your air is impeding the instruments ability to do what it needs to do which is why we have said practice is important and to make sure that you're practicing so that you can have the proper technique. The reason that this will help you is that it is going to make sure that the instrument sounds as good as it can and that it can sound the way that you're needing it to sound.

Learning a new instrument can be very daunting when you first start out because it's a lot of information to take in and it's a lot of information that you'll need to absorb but by following the information and making sure that you have the proper knowledge of what you need to do and how you need to use this instrument, you'll be able to play it much better. The best part? Knowing how to fix problems is going to help you be able to have fun playing the music and when you begin to play and you'll know how to fix or tweak any issues.

With anything that you attempt the more practice you do for yourself, the better that you will be. By practicing your playing, you'll be able to play really fun songs and more quickly than if you didn't practice. You will also be able to have more fun with this instrument. So by practicing, you're going to make sure that you'll be able to have more fun when you're learning how to do this and learn how to play fun songs.

Let's Start Playing !

Now that we've gone over the basics we're going to tell you how you can start playing your instrument and learning how to play it.

We have talked about how you need to place the recorder in your mouth and what not to do and we've told you that only the tip of the mouthpiece should be in your mouth.

- Press down very gently with your upper lip you can try whispering to yourself mmmm and this will put your mouth into the correct position.

- Be careful not to let your teeth or your tongue touch the mouthpiece. Just your lips.

- Make sure that your lips are nice and firm around the mouthpiece and you want to make sure that you are not closing and opening your mouth on each individual note. The reason for this is that it will cause air leaking if you do this.

- Make sure that your lips are firm so that you're avoiding air leaks instead. Remember that air leaks and bubbles are two things that we really need to avoid because they're going to affect how your instrument sounds. You want to produce a sound that is clear and not a sound that squeaky.

- Blow soft and with a steady airstream. Only a little air is required because this is a very small instrument so if you blow too hard it's going to produce a very obnoxious noise that you might not like.

- Be sure also to use the steamy window trick. Blow on your hand as if you're steaming up your car window without someone near you hearing. You don't want them to hear you blow into the instrument. The air should be warm but it should not be heard. Blow the same way into your recorder. You are going to start the breath by whispering the word tu. When you do this, this is called tonguing and your teacher will explain more about this in the future once you begin taking lessons. Remember, we've also said where to place your tongue on your teeth and the sounds that you should be making so that you're able to tongue your notes properly.

- If you squeak remember that you might be blowing too hard. You need a very steady airstream.

- Another thing to remember is that your fingers need to be covering the holes correctly. The next step that you will need to learn is how to read a fingering chart and to know your instrument.

- Remember that your left thumb is going to be on the back hole and your first three fingers are going to be on the first three holes. Your pinky is touching nothing.

The next thing we told you about where to stick your next thumb and remember that your first, second, third and fourth fingers will cover the holes that are on the bottom.

When you're reading a fingering chart you will know that the holes are either white or black. If the hole is black, that means your finger should be down and covering the hole. If the hole is white it means uncovered.

Occasionally on a fingering chart you will see a hole that is half black and half white. These are called half-hole notes.

So when you see a note like this, you need to move your left thumb so it only covers half of the bottom hole. So this means that your leaving the hole half open.

You may find it easier to bend your left thumb so that the tip of your thumb nail is pressing into the middle of the hole. The knowledge in this chapter is really going to be able to help you with your notes because that's what we're going to go over next.

The Fingering Chart

We will list the notes one by one and explain very carefully how to cover your recorders holes and when your fingers need to be uncovered so that you're able to understand which fingers go where and how to place them correctly so that you can learn the notes correctly and as easily as possible.

There is a set of notes that are specific for your left hand and others that are suited for your right.

As such we explain which notes are for your left hand and which of your right hand and we will also go over what holes need to be covered and what holes need to be uncovered for each of these notes.

By explaining exactly where your fingers need to be you'll be able to begin playing these notes easier which will make the learning process easier as well.

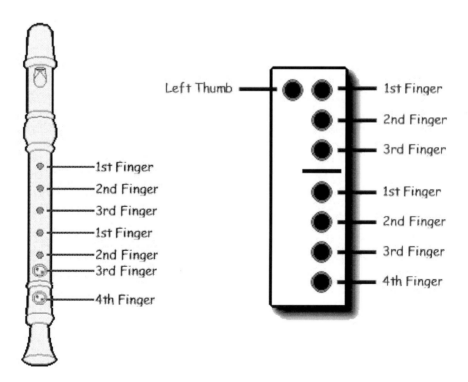

If the hole is black, your finger should press down and cover that hole. If the hole is white, should be left uncovered.

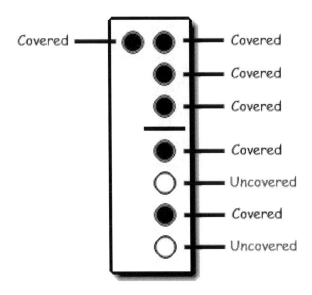

If the hole is one-half black and one-half white, it's called "Half-Hole" notes.

In this case, you should move your left thumb so that it covers only the bottom half of the hole. You may find it easier to bend your left thumb so that the tip of your thumbnail is pressing into the middle of the hole.

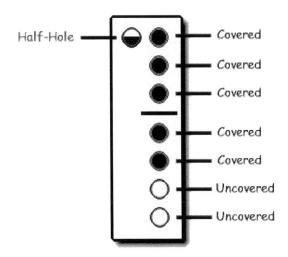

23

How to Play Notes

Closed Hole

Open Hole

C

In the C note every hole covered

Low D

A low D is at the bottom of the bar and every hole will be covered except your right hand pinky. That hole will be uncovered.

Low E

A low E is every finger covered except the third finger and the fourth finger of your right hand.

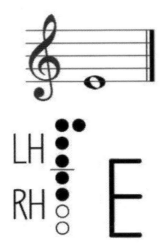

Low F

A low F is every finger covered except the second finger on your right hand.

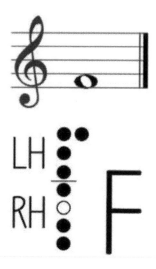

F# (F sharp)

An F sharp is a little different. You will notice that a note is sharp if it has a number symbol that looks like this. #. An F# is every finger covered except your first finger on your right hand and your fourth finger on your right hand. These two should be uncovered.

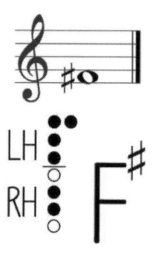

G

A G is every finger covered except your right hand. No fingers on your right hand will be covering any holes, just your left hand.

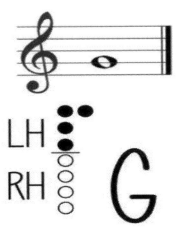

A

So the A is in the second space and this has the first and second fingers of your left hand and your back thumb covered, all of the other holes are uncovered which means that the third finger of your left hand is uncovered and there are no fingers of your right hand covering any holes at all.

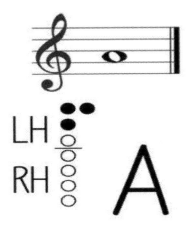

B♭

You can tell a note is flat because it will have a line and a curve symbol next to it to make it look like a small B. For a B flat you need the first finger on your left hand covered along with your back thumb covered and the third finger of your left hand and the first finger of your right hand covered. So then your second finger of your left hand is uncovered and the second, third and fourth fingers of your right hand are uncovered.

B

The only fingers you will be covering for this note is your first finger on your left hand and your thumb on your left hand. So for this note it's those first two fingers. Everything else is uncovered. So the second and third finger of your left hand are uncovered and all four fingers of your right hand are uncovered.

C'

To play the note you need to uncover your first finger on your left hand, your third finger on your left hand and every finger on your right hand. The only fingers that should be covered are your second finger on your left hand and your back thumb.

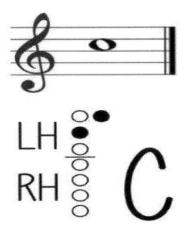

D

This D is on the fourth line of the bar and the only finger that should be covered is the second finger of your left hand, the first, third and back thumb are uncovered and all of the fingers on your right hand are uncovered

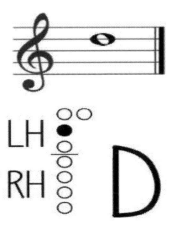

Rhythm

Rhythm is very important and it's one of the ways to extend the duration of a sound or of silence. What we mean by this is if you have a half note, a half note is two beats long. So the note will hold for one beat and then another. A whole note is four beats. So it would hot for one beat, then two, three, and four.

For this example, we're going to use a half note which we've said is two beats long. If it is a dotted half note we would hold the note for two beats plus half of its original value which is one beat. so we would hold that note for a total of three beats long. This is two beats plus the additional beat. If we did a dotted quarter note, a quarter note is one beat long and then a dotted quarter we would play and hold that note for the original value plus half of the original value. So if you had a dotted quarter note, you would hold it for one and a half beats because that's the length of a quarter note and an eighth of a note.

You will be able to see these because the note will have a dot next to it. A semi breve which is a whole note with a dot is six beats. This is how you know that it's one of the notes that is going to need extra beats. A dotted semi breve which is a dotted whole note is for four beats plus half of the original value. Half of the original value of a whole note is two beats so you would be doing four plus two which equals six. So you would hold that note for six beats.

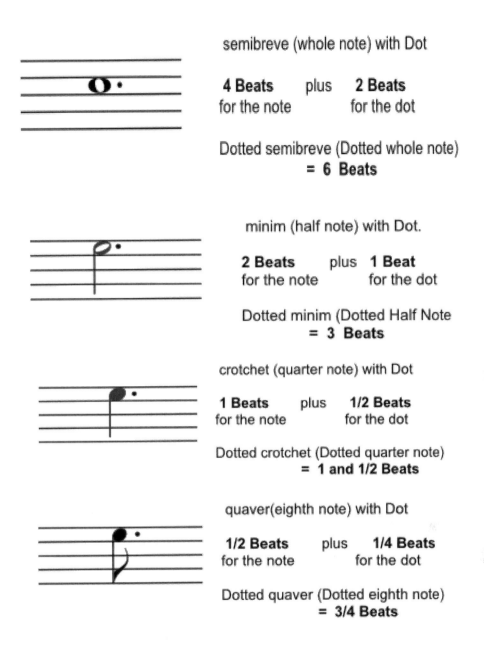

semibreve (whole note) with Dot

4 Beats   plus   **2 Beats**
for the note   for the dot

Dotted semibreve (Dotted whole note)
= 6 Beats

minim (half note) with Dot.

2 Beats   plus   **1 Beat**
for the note   for the dot

Dotted minim (Dotted Half Note
= 3 Beats

crotchet (quarter note) with Dot

1 Beats   plus   **1/2 Beats**
for the note   for the dot

Dotted crotchet (Dotted quarter note)
= 1 and 1/2 Beats

quaver(eighth note) with Dot

1/2 Beats   plus   **1/4 Beats**
for the note   for the dot

Dotted quaver (Dotted eighth note)
= 3/4 Beats

If you wanted to do a half note that is dotted that would be two beats plus one beat. So you will hold that note for three beats instead of two. This would be the normal count plus another beat. If you had a crochet, which is a quarter note with a dot. That is one beat for the note plus half of it for the dot. So you would have one and a half beats. Using the examples we've given you is going to help you understand how you can start with your rhythm. All you have to remember is that when you have the dot, a dot increases a note by half of the value. Now that we've talked about rhythm, we can talk about beats.

We are going to use your heart to help you understand beats. Do you know how to feel your heartbeat? What you would do is place the first two fingers of either hand on either the left or right part of your neck and you'll feel your heartbeat. This heartbeat is also called your pulse. Each pulse of your heart is a beat. So if your heart is in your chest beating and you have placed your fingers at your throat to feel it imagine you feel a thump four times. So each thump is a beat if you felt four thumps, thump, thump, thump, thump. This equals four beats. Beat, beat, beat, beat.

Music has a steady beat just like your heart. Each pulse of the music is called a beat. If you tap your fingers on a table with a steady beat you can follow the notes with each tap. So if you had single notes In four four time you would go tap tap tap tap. Or one, two, three, and four. Each tap would only be for one beat where is if you had a shorter note your tapping would be faster. The beat is a regular, reoccurring and steady pulse. It enables you to keep your counting on time and it causes the listener to clap your hands or move your body in time with the beat. You'll notice when people play music they tend to tap there toes or move their bodies as well.

The beat is also going to provide the foundation for your rhythm and music. There is a musical rule that there's always a bar line at the end of every staff and there's always a bar line at the end of every measure or bar. Bar lines are not typically placed at the beginning of the music or after the treble signature or time signatures.

There is a double bar at the end of every piece or section and it is made up of one thin line and one thick line. The thick line is always on the outside. If you're able to utilize this to your benefit you will be able to understand things like rhythm as well as the notes that you're gong to be learning and how to play them as well as how to move your fingers in the proper manner.

Examples

- Tap your fingers on the desk with a steady bear. Follow the notes below with each tap. Each quarter note gets one tap of your fingers. On this staff each quarter note gets one beat.

- Now tap it again, but this time, tap a little louder on the first note in each measure.

  In this example, there are four quarter note beats in each measure. Half notes and eighth notes can be used as a beat, too.

- Three half note beats in these measures.

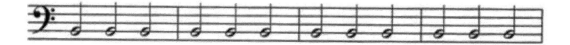

- Six eighth note beats in these measures.

Bar lines

Notes are easier to read when they are divided into groups. Notes are divided into equal groups with lines called bar lines. Bar lines are lines that divide the staff into equal parts.

The area (group of notes) between the two (2) bar lines are called the measures or bars.

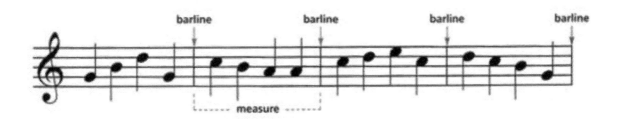

Musi

1) At the end of every staff, there is always a bar line

2) At the end of every measure/bar, there is always a bar line .

3) The bar lines are not generally placed at the beginning of the music after the clef, or the Key signature or time signature.

4) At the end of every piece or section there is a double bar line.

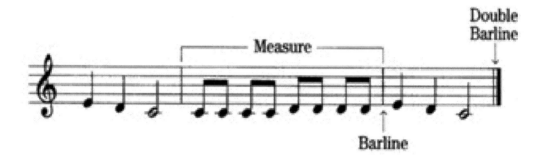

Mapping between musical notation and Tablature fingering position

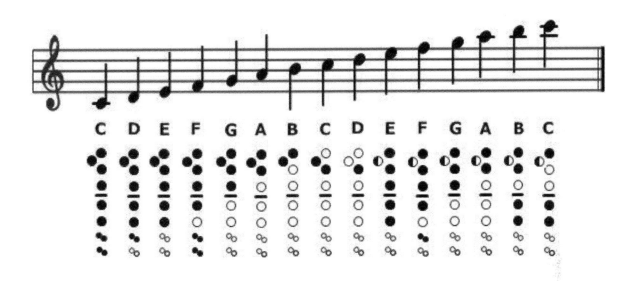

Time To Practice

Now that we know how the notes are fingered properly and what you need to do to be able to play them properly, it's time to practice. The first thing that you're going to need to understand is that there's a difference between left-handed notes and right-handed notes and now it's time to learn these notes so you can see the difference. There are sequences for these notes as well. They are not very long which makes practicing easier because they are only a handful of notes long.

These sequences are what we will be listing below because knowing the sequence is going to be able to help you figure out which notes you need to learn first. It is easier for beginners to learn the left-handed notes first before learning the right-handed notes. The left-handed notes that you need only require you to only use four fingers but once you start learning the right-handed notes, you will be using eight. As this is twice as many as you were using before, it is a bit harder and that is why you should learn the left-handed notes first because you're only using half of the fingers.

This is how we're going to be setting up this chapter we're going to list the left-handed notes first because they're easier and then the right handed notes once you've gained a good understanding of the left-handed no   The first note that we're going to try in this chapter is the B. To play this note place your fingers over the proper holes.

Cover the hole on the back with your left thumb and then cover the top hole which is the closest to the mouthpiece with the index finger of your left hand. You should be using the flat part of your finger as we discussed before and your right thumb will not be used for covering the hole. Only your left thumb will be used for covering the hole. The right thumb is simply used to help support the instrument. This is especially important if you're using a larger recorder. Now you're going to blow into the instrument with the sound and breath that we've discussed earlier and you should hear a B note.

Once you were able to successfully play a B note, you can practice until you feel that you've got it dow. From there you can start practicing the other notes as well. The trick of some of the notes is that some are going to be lower and some will be higher. If you see these notes on paper or in a book and it has a tick then you will be able to know the difference between a high note and a low note because of the tick and the sound of course as a second way to tell. When you are seeing a tick you will see that these notes are different.

If you see a note that has a tick after it this is an indication that the note is a high note. If you have a low note be aware that low notes will not have a tick at all. Very high notes are different as well because they will usually have two ticks. The notes that are left-handed notes are the notes that use only the fingers of the left hand. Your left hand little finger is never used. As we said in the previous chapter each finger has a hole assigned to each one. So each finger has a specific hole.

Each finger only ever covers that one hole and because of this you should keep your fingers close to the holes even when the holes are not being covered. The ideal situation for your fingers is that you should place each finger about a centimeter over the hole and ready to cover the hole when it is needed. Having your fingers in place can take training but it will help you play better because your fingers are in the right spot and your getting used to covering and uncovering the holes and how to hold your fingers on uncovered notes.

Some left-handed notes are the following. The B note, the A note, the G note, the C note, and the D note. When you're practicing it can be very beneficial to practice them in that order. Play B, then A, then G, then C and finally D. This order ensures that your fingers are in all the right places. With these five notes, you can play simple tunes in the key of G. There is another sequence of notes that you can do with these notes as well to play music.

If you do this, in another sequence try playing the notes G then the note A, the next would be C, the following note is B and the last would be D. This will form the sequence do, re, me, fa, so. This is a popular sequence in music and familiar with many. A good example of a left-handed tune would be Mary had a little lamb. This is a familiar song and it is very good for a beginner to learn. Although the next chapter has easy tunes for you to learn there are two different ways that you can play Mary had a little lamb. As such we will list the first version here and the second in the next chapter.

Mary had a little lamb
The first way to play Mary had a little lamb is by playing the following notes:

B A G A B B B A A A D D D A G A B B A A B A G

All of the notes in this version are notes that are left-handed notes. Another example of a fun tune that is easy to learn and is full of left handed notes would be

When the Saints go marching in
This is also a song that many people have heard many times in their childhood and is a great song to learn, it helps with their fingering and breathing. The notes for this song would be the following.

G B C D G B C D G B C D B G B A B B A G G B D D C B C D

A B A G

This will let you play the song and have fun understanding left-handed notes.

Right-handed notes on the other hand are different and the will utilize different fingers. You use the thumb in your left hand but you don't on your right, you use your right pinkie but not your left. So it can take a minute to get used to it.

Once you feel comfortable using the notes that only use your left hand you can start incorporating more notes and begin the process of learning more notes that use the right hand as well as the bottom holes of the recorder.

Remember that we said each finger on your hand is going to have a specific hole and you will use all of your fingers on your right hand but you will never use your thumb because your thumb is the stabilizer.

Your thumb should press against the back of the recorder and the fingers of your right hand would be numbered the fourth, fifth, sixth and seventh fingers.

Your right fingers are how you will be playing different notes with your right hand and covering different . This is just like you would with your left hand but the notes are a bit different. You will be playing a D and an F sharp which will have the symbol we showed you before.

Just as the other notes came in a sequence, you can practice each of these with a G that you already know in the order of the following notes. G note, then the E note, followed by the D note and then the F sharp. When you can play all of these notes you have the notes that you need to play a multitude of different songs and expand your knowledge to challenge yourself and learn more songs that are fun and good for notes, and covering the holes and getting used to the instrument. This will take practice however, because it is difficult for us to get all of the holes covered exactly the way that you need them to. Some examples of a right handed song would be twinkle twinkle little star.

Song Book

Happy Birthday

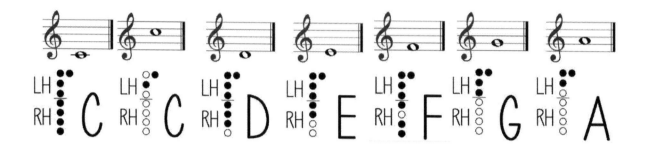

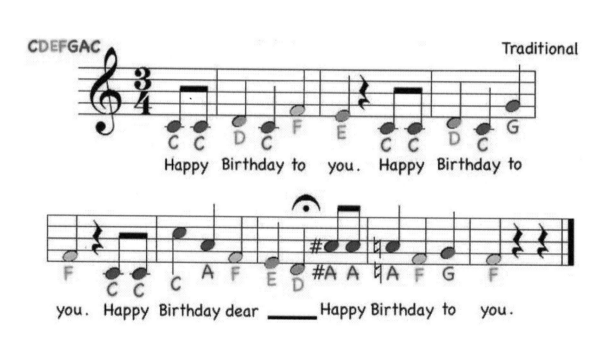

Twinkle, Twinkle Little Star

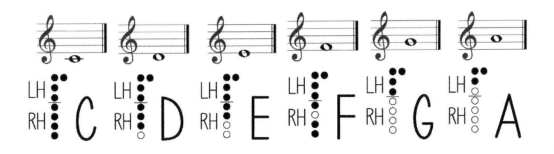

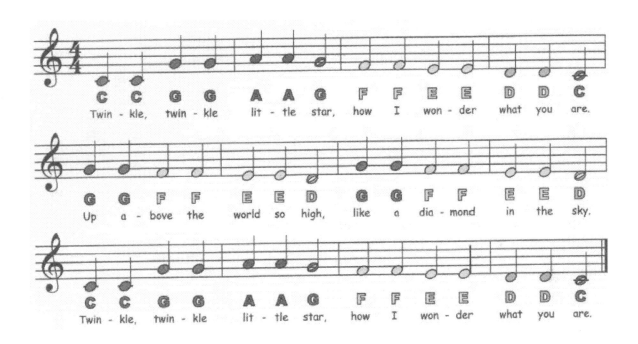

Twin - kle, twin - kle lit - tle star, how I won - der what you are.

Up a - bove the world so high, like a dia - mond in the sky.

Twin - kle, twin - kle lit - tle star, how I won - der what you are.

Row Row Row Your Boat

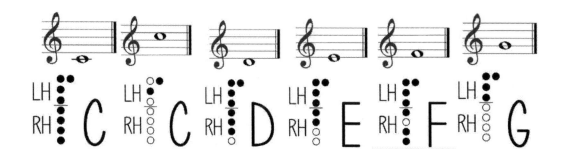

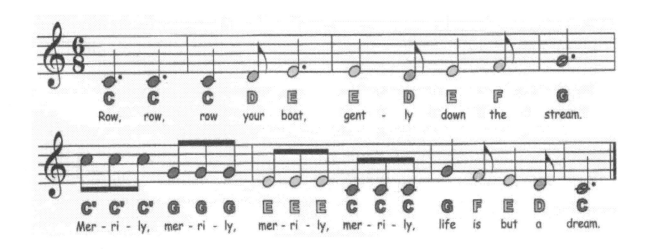

Frere Jacques

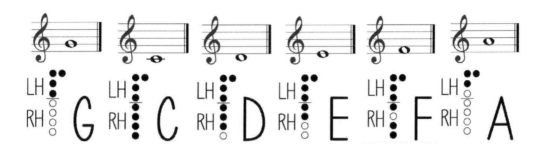

The Old Gray Mare

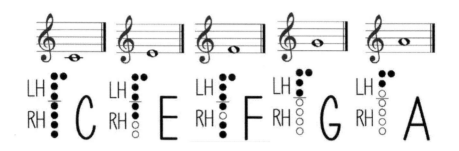

The Muffin Man

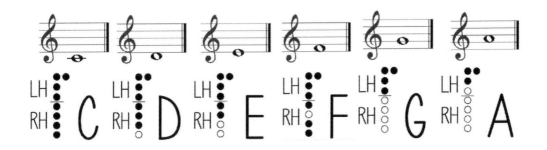

There's a Hole in the Bucket

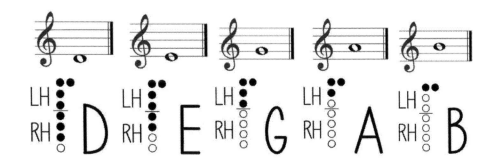

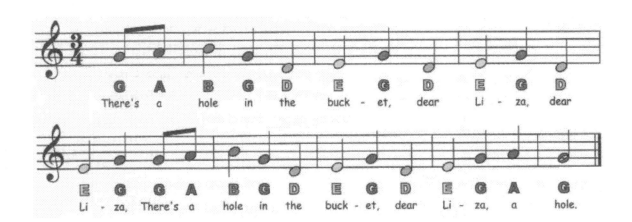

This Old Man

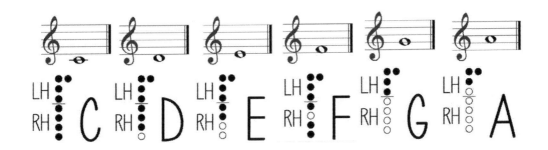

Hush, Little Baby

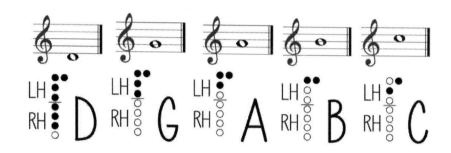

Mary Had a Little Lamb

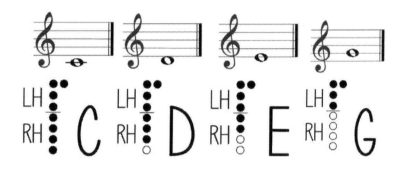

London Bridge

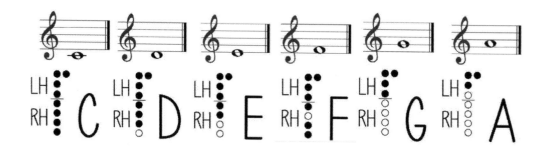

Old Mac Donald Had a Farm

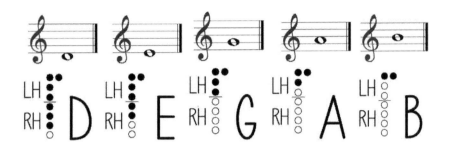

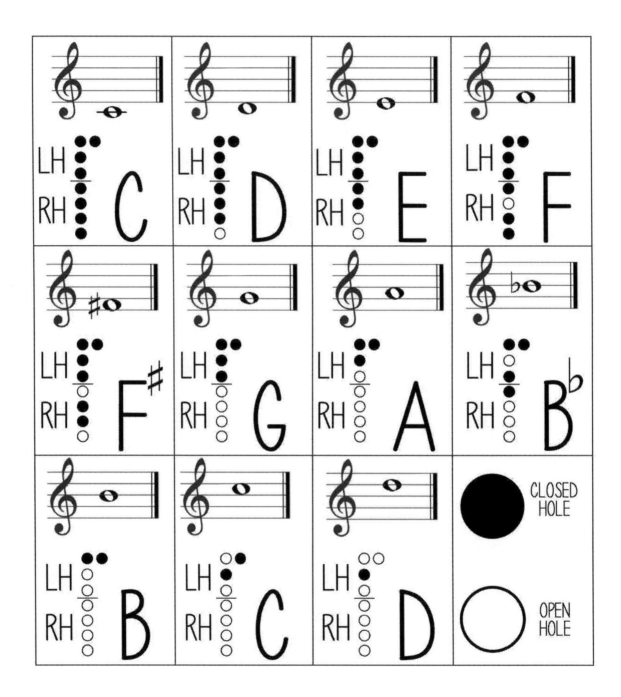

Care your Recorder

Keep in mind the following important things:

1) **To never ever touch the labium**. The labium is the sharp edge of your instrument that produces the sound. The labium is going to look a little like a ramp with a sharp edge. It's cut into the instrument right after the mouthpiece. If you damage this piece the entire instrument is now rendered useless. A side note, this piece is very delicate.

   If the wind way gets blocked with moisture do not poke anything into it. This could damage the labium. You need to cover the window without touching the labium and then blow hard. This should be enough to clear it. However, if the wind way is seriously blocked and that doesn't work then what you need to do is take off the head joint. Put your hand over the end where it joins onto the body of the instrument and put your mouth over the window and then blow. If this still doesn't work, then you need to poke a feather into the wind way. This will not damage the labium if it accidentally touches it so you won't break your instrument or break it.

2) **Use a gentle twisting action**: when you're putting your recorder together or taking it apart you need to use a gentle twisting action to prevent the joints from being damaged.

3) **Dry it**: When you are playing moisture usually condenses inside the recorder. This is natural. So what you're going to have to do after each use is dry it. Doing this is really good practice for plastic recorders, but it's essential if you have a

wooden recorder because as we said above no water can get anywhere near it. Your saliva is not as dangerous as water but it is still dangerous to the instrument so you'll have to make sure that you are drying it out.

4) **Use linseed oil**: If your joints are cork then you need to apply a little cork grease to make sure that you're keeping them supple. The suitable oil and grease that you need is available in any music shop that you go into and it is recommended that you buy them from a music shop because they have the proper ones that you need. Remember, when you're taking care of your instrument you can only use certain oils and trying to use a different one may damage your instrument. The music shop also has books, along with sheet music and even tutors that can be able to help take your musical ability and interests further. This is especially beneficial if you want to become a professional later on.

Conclusion

This is the book that you need for understanding how to play the recorder and how to learn to play it simply and effectively. The information that you will find in this book will help you learn the instruments pieces and the proper technique so that you can make the instrument last as long as possible. Despite being made of plastic, these are not toys or cheap. They need care and they need you to be able to blow into them in the proper manner. Blowing into them wrong means squeaking and high pitches that are incorrect. Blowing into it properly can make all the difference. It is little things like these that you need to know and that we are making sure you will be able to do here.

We have the information that you need on how to learn the notes that you need and how to work your fingers so that you will be able to make sure that your covering the holes of your instrument correctly. This and proper air will ensure the sound is coming out perfectly. This is exactly what you will need to learn to play properly and it is what you will learn from this book here. We offer a variety of songs that you love and have heard all your life. This makes the instrument fun and interesting.

Everyone loves to make music and let it be a part of you which is what learning this instrument will do for you. Music can be a great benefit for your mind and spirit and this instrument dates back hundreds of years. Imagine how much influence this has had over musical culture. Music also helps improve brain power and can help excell you in the academic world as well. It is also great for inspiring your inner creativity by allowing you the freedom to learn new songs, write your own music and have fun doing both. This will help you as you get older and help you in life.

With the knowledge in this book you will be armed with the ability to be able to learn to play simple songs but have the skills and the drive to learn harder ones as well. The recorder is a great instrument to learn to give you a great confidence boost and learn that you can develop skills on your own. It also teaches you skills that you will need later in life such as patience. When your playing in a group you always have to wait on others and wait for the person in charge to tell you to play. Being able to play in a group also lets you see how you can work together and make friends while making awesome music together.

Use this book and it's tips and learn to make wonderful music and harmonies that you can enjoy and use to your emotional and mental benefits. Start with songs like Twinkle Twinkle Little Star and then build up to things like Jingle Bells. We offer songs of all types and genres in this book and we pay special attention to the notes and placement of your hands. This book will make sure your playing in no time!

Manufactured by Amazon.ca
Bolton, ON